BRITAIN IN OLD PHOTOGRAPHS

BEDFORDSHIRE AT WAR

NIGEL LUTT

SUTTON PUBLISHING LIMITED

Sutton Publishing Limited
Phoenix Mill · Thrupp · Stroud
Gloucestershire · GL5 2BU

First published 1997
in association with the County Record Office,
Bedfordshire County Council

Cover photographs: *front*; air raid on Bedford,
23 July 1942: *back*; soldiers washing clothes at
Luton, *c.* 1916.

British Library Cataloguing in Publication Data
A catalogue record for this book is available from the
British Library.

ISBN 0-7509-1433-5

Typeset in 10/12 Perpetua.
Typesetting and origination by
Sutton Publishing Limited.
Printed in Great Britain by
Ebenezer Baylis, Worcester.

A war correspondent snaps an airman of the United States Air Force helping with the harvest near
Bletsoe, August 1943.

CONTENTS

INDEX

Photographers and film crew turned out in force when Princess Elizabeth visited Thurleigh airfield to christen a B-17 bomber Rose of York in 1944.

INTRODUCTION

Wars have had a profound effect on the people and landscape of Bedfordshire, particularly in the years since 1914. That legacy is still with us today – in the reminders provided by war memorials and wartime defences – and in the memories of those who lived through those times. Old pictures are another part of this legacy, and this book brings together over 180 of the best 'images of war'.

Bedfordshire at War in Old Photographs is the second book produced by Sutton Publishing in association with Bedfordshire Record Office. The first volume, *Bedfordshire at Work*, was published in 1994. Once again I have drawn heavily on the extensive picture collection held by the Record Office, but I owe a special debt of gratitude to Luton Museum for the use of some of their material relating to Luton and the south of the county.

Photography has only been with us for about 150 years, so before then we have to rely on paintings, engravings and documents for information. Some examples from the period *c.* 1685–1850 are in the chapter on the pre-camera age (Section One). We have to wait until the French Revolution and Napoleonic Wars of 1793–1815 for the first pictures of local soldiers (see pp. 12, 14, 17, 18) and most of these, as you would expect, are officers from gentry families. In the 1850s photography became more widespread and the pictures taken by Roger Fenton, a war correspondent during the Crimean War, demonstrated the possibilities of photography on the battlefield. Closer to home, the formation of corps of rifle volunteers in Bedfordshire in 1859–60 roughly coincided with the arrival of commercial photographers in the county (see pp. 25–6) and this meant that local part-time soldiers could have portraits taken cheaply. During the remainder of Victoria's reign (Section Two) photographs gradually become more plentiful. The amount of material available for the South African War of 1899–1902 in particular (see pp. 32–9) reflects just how much this campaign, in which the Boer farmers kept the might of the British army at bay, impinged on the public consciousness.

The following period up to 1914 (Section Three) was one of uneasy peace, marked by some important developments such as the creation of the Territorial Army in 1908. The First World War (Section Four) is notable for the large number of surviving photographs reflecting the age of total war in the rise of mass armies and the activities of civilians on the home front. There are some interesting pictures of this period, but thanks in part to the influence of censorship they do tend to offer a sanitised view of the war, an image of parades and formal portraits far removed from the reality.

Between the First and Second World Wars (Section Five) Bedfordshire celebrated the peace (pp. 71–4) and mourned its losses of over 5,300 men in action by erecting war memorials in the towns and villages (pp. 75–7). Luton Town Hall was burned down on Peace Day 1919 in one of the most notorious events in Bedfordshire's history (p. 74). In the interwar period the Bedfordshire and Hertfordshire Regiment resumed its role of policing the Empire and served in Shanghai in 1927–8 (p. 79) as well as in Palestine in the late 1930s (p. 81).

When the Second World War (Section Six) broke out in 1939 press photographers were on hand to make a record and this book includes pictures from the *Bedfordshire Times* collection (held at the Record Office) and the *Luton News* archive (at Luton Museum). These sources, together with the work of amateur photographers, combine to give a comprehensive view of the home front in Bedfordshire, everything from evacuees to air raids and celebrities to salvage. Away from the home front Bedfordshire was involved in one of the biggest disasters of the war. The 5th Battalion Bedfordshire and Hertfordshire Regiment (TA) was part of the allied force which surrendered to the Japanese on the fall of Singapore in February 1942. This volume includes two water-colours painted by prisoners-of-war (p. 104) under conditions of great hardship.

The release of Bedfordshire's prisoners-of-war at the end of hostilities gave added zest to the peace celebrations which followed in 1945–6 (Section Seven). Street parties, processions and carnivals were the order of the day, but after the euphoria died away people had to face the legacy of war (Section Eight) including the loss of loved ones, continued rationing and a shortage of housing. The last fifty years has eased the personal hardship caused by war, but local landmarks (pp. 125–6) and Remembrance Day ceremonies (p. 127) provide salutary reminders of the past. I hope this book will prove to be a similar reminder of how wars have shaped the history of Bedfordshire and its people over the last 300 years. My thanks go to everyone who has donated or loaned us photographs over the years and made this volume possible.

Nigel Lutt
Bedfordshire Record Office

THE PRE-CAMERA AGE
TO *c.* 1850

Here lieth y^e body of
Lievt^{e}nant PHILIP MONOUX
who was slaine in his Majesties
Service (King Iames y^e Second)
in y^e Forrest of Rouse in Somerset=
Shire, against y^e Rebels of y^e Late
Duke of Monmouth Iune y^e 19°
in y^e year 1685°
in the 29° year of his Age .
He was first buried in y^e Church
of Chard in Somerset Shire from
thence removed at y^e desire and
Charge of his Nephew S^r. Philip
Monoux Barron^t & Layed in this
place with this Stone over him
in Memory of him .

This memorial stone in the chancel of Wootton church is a reminder of the last battle fought on English soil.
Philip Monoux was killed in a skirmish with the Duke of Monmouth's forces, but on 6 July 1685 the rebels
were decisively defeated at Sedgemoor by the army of James II. The third baronet, another Philip Monoux,
arranged for his uncle's body to be returned to Wootton.

The 16th Foot or Bedfordshire Regiment was raised in October 1688 by James II in an effort to muster loyal regiments and thereby counter the threat from William of Orange. This reconstructed scene, painted by C.C.P. Lawson in about 1938, depicts recruiting in Reading. The regiment was known by the

names of its successive colonels until numbered 16th in 1751, and only became the Bedfordshire
Regiment in 1881.

Sergeant-Major Edward Furnival of the Bedfordshire Militia standing near St Peter's Church, Bedford, *c*. 1790. He was appointed sergeant in the Leighton Buzzard Company when the county militia was raised in March 1760 during the Seven Years' War and was promoted sergeant-major in April 1779 during the war with America. He died at Bedford in March 1800. His three sons, Thomas junior, James Hinton and Samuel, were all sergeants in their father's regiment.

Bedford Volunteers.

ALL Persons who have Signed their Names to the BEDFORD VOLUNTEER CORPS, or who intend to become Members of that Body, are requested to attend on *St. Peter's Green*, in *Bedford*, on WEDNESDAY EVENING next, the 10th of *August*, at 6 o'Clock precisely, for a General Muster,——Punctuality to the time appointed is most particularly requested.

Every Volunteer belonging to the Town of *Bedford*, will be pleased to repair, as soon as he shall appear on the Green, to the Station which will be marked for his Parish, and those from any of the Parishes without the Town, to a Station which will be appointed for them.

By the Voluntary Exertions of His People, may the King Triumph over His Enemies !!!

AUGUST, 1803. ISAAC ELGER, MAYOR.

After the short-lived peace of Amiens in 1801–1802, war was declared again between England and France in 1803. In the wake of the renewed hostilities the Bedford volunteers were mustered on St Peter's Green.

Major John Harvey (1772–1819) of Ickwell Bury, Northill, commanded the Bedfordshire Dismounted Horse Artillery during the Napoleonic Wars. He raised the regiment in 1803 in the face of renewed threats of invasion by France.

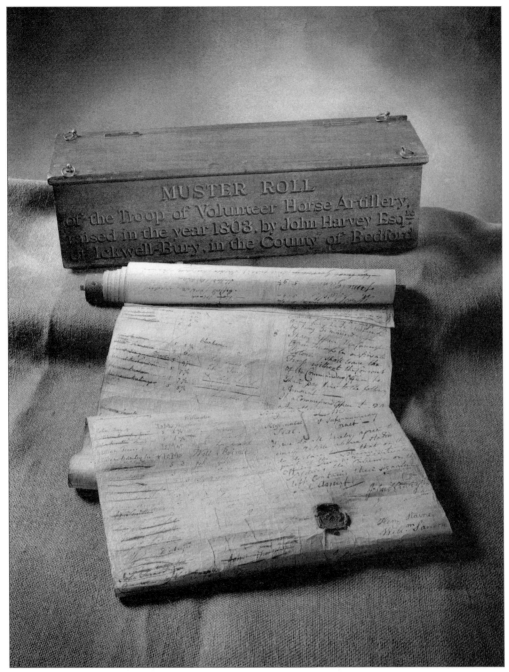

The muster roll of the Bedfordshire Dismounted Horse Artillery with its original box. The roll gives the names, heights and signatures or marks of over 200 men from Northill and district who enrolled between 1803 and 1809, when the regiment was amalgamated with the local militia. The document also includes the regulations drawn up for the corps in June 1805 which introduced fines ranging from sixpence for lateness or inattention in the ranks, to a shilling for discharging firearms when off-duty and a hefty £20 for officers leaving the troop without permission.

A Volunteer for the Navy

WANTED for the Parifhes of SHARNBROOK, SOULDROP, WIMMINGTON, and PUDDINGTON, in the County of Bedford, ONE able bodied YOUNG MAN, from Sixteen to Forty-five Years of Age, to ferve in His MAJESTY'S NAVY during the War, or Three Months after.

Any Perfon qualified, and having only One Child, by applying to the *Churchwardens* or *Overfeers* of the Poor of either of the faid Parifhes, on or before the 16th. Day of APRIL, fhall, upon being regularly excepted & approved of, receive a BOUNTY of

TWENTY-SIX GUINEAS,

And a GOLD-LACED HAT, JACKET and TROWSERS, without any Dedution from the faid Parifhes, with a regular MAINTENANCE from GOVERNMENT, and his WHOLE SHARE of PRIZE MONEY, whatever it may be.

Printed by W. Smith, Stationer, Bookfeller, Binder and Paperhanger.

Advertisement for a volunteer for the Navy offering various inducements to join up, *c.* 1803. Sometimes less gentle methods were used. Thomas Travell of Ampthill moved to London and was press-ganged on to HMS *Veteran*, dying in 1807.

In the Name of God Amen

I, Thomas Bradshaw late first Lieutenant belonging to his Majesty ship Pearl

The will of Thomas Bradshaw of Leighton Buzzard, formerly a 1st Lieutenant on HMS *Pearl*, shows warships in action. Bradshaw made his will in 1766, leaving his property to his wife Ann. He later became a Quaker and died in 1810.

William Astell MP (1774–1847) of Everton Park, Colonel of the Royal East Anglia Volunteers, in a portrait by M. Acher Shee, 1808. He was a son-in-law of John Harvey of Ickwell who raised the Bedfordshire Dismounted Horse Artillery (see page 14).

John Pym, born in 1795, was the fourth son of Francis and Ann Pym of Hasells Hall, Sandy. He became a cornet (a junior officer in a troop of cavalry who carried the flag or standard) in the 13th Light Dragoons in 1811 and a lieutenant the following year when this water-colour was painted. John Pym was killed at the battle of Waterloo on 18 June 1815.

John Thomas Brooks of Flitwick (1794–1858) as a cornet in the 14th Light Dragoons, c. 1815. Brooks did not see active service. In 1816 he married Mary Hatfield and left both London and the army to live at Flitwick Manor, now a restaurant.

The Dunstable Downs shutter telegraph by the artist George Shepherd, 1819. The shutter telegraph system was devised in 1795 and taken up by the Admiralty who needed to pass messages quickly between their headquarters in London and the major naval stations at Plymouth, Portsmouth, Deal and Great Yarmouth. The shutters on the wooden frame were pulled open or closed by a rope or chain and the different combinations displayed could represent letters, code words or numbers. The Dunstable telegraph was constructed in 1807 as part of the 146 mile route between London and Great Yarmouth, but it was abandoned in 1814 in favour of a simpler semaphore system. No trace of the Dunstable telegraph survives today and this view of it after closure is the only illustration known.

Lieutenant Colonel Thomas Potter Macqueen of the Bedfordshire Yeomanry, *c.* 1824. The Yeomanry was formed during the French invasion scare of 1794 and by 1797 it had squadrons at Bedford, Odell, Old Warden and Woburn. The regiment was disbanded in 1827. Thomas Potter Macqueen (1791–1854) enjoyed a colourful political career, serving as Member of Parliament for Bedfordshire in 1826–1830, and encouraging the colonization of New South Wales in the 1820s and 1830s.

Bedfordshire Light Infantry Militia private as painted by William Cooper Cooper in 1853. The militia had been reorganised in 1852 thanks to the threat posed by a revitalised France under Napoleon III, Napoleon Bonaparte's nephew.

William Cooper Cooper of Toddington (1810–1898) was a noted local historian and one of the early pioneers of photography in Bedfordshire. He was an officer in the Bedfordshire Militia between 1846 and 1858 and painted some interesting water-colours during his service.

William Cooper Cooper, then a captain in the Bedfordshire Militia, painted this water-colour of the interior of his hut at Aldershot in 1855, shortly before the regiment moved to Ireland on garrison duty during the Crimean War. The accommodation is fairly spartan and includes a dresser and table for his personal belongings, and a washstand.

SOLDIERS OF THE QUEEN, *c.* 1850–1901

*The Russian cannon from the Crimean War
(1854–1856) which once stood on Bedford Embankment
near Russell Park, pictured in about 1900. It was
scrapped by Bedford Corporation in
a salvage drive in 1942.*

John Hatfield Brooks (1824–1907) of Flitwick Manor, son of John Thomas Brooks (see page 18), as a captain in the 1st European Light Cavalry at Allahabad, India in September 1858. Brooks served during the Sikh Wars, including the battle of Chillianwallah in 1849, and in the Indian Mutiny of 1857–8, before returning to his Flitwick estates in 1859.

The Ninth Bedfordshire Volunteer Rifle Corps at camp in Ampthill Park, with the ruins of Houghton House in the background, *c.* 1865. The Corps were founded in 1859–60 to counter the threat from France: their descendants are the present day Territorial Army. These two views are by Cundall, Downs and Co. of Bedford, one of the first firms of commercial photographers in the county.

Studio portrait of a soldier in the Bedfordshire Volunteer Rifle Corps, *c.* 1865. The uniform was far from popular. Captain John Thomas Green of the Woburn Company wrote to his commanding officer, the Duke of Bedford, to complain that 'the risk run by anyone who wears our present uniform of incurring public ridicule . . . has proved sufficient to deter men from entering our ranks'.

The Victorian barracks at Kempston, the Regimental Depot of the 16th Foot or Bedfordshire Regiment, were built in 1875–6 at the cost of about £50,000. The first troops arrived on 29 May 1877 and over the next sixty years thousands of men were trained here. During the Second World War the barracks were used mainly as a convalescent centre, other functions having been transferred to Bury St. Edmunds. The photographs show the building in about 1910 (above) and at night, c. 1955.

Both regular battalions of the Bedfordshire Regiment served for long periods in India in the last quarter of the nineteenth century. Captain John Stanley Lightfoot is shown having tea with Lieutenant H.C. Franks (in striped blazer) at Ramandroog in 1890. The officers were in charge of a party of one hundred young soldiers of the 2nd Battalion recently joined from England who were sent to the Ramandroog Convalescent Depot to become acclimatised. In the lower picture, 1st Battalion signallers pose with their equipment at the Secunderabad Camp of Exercise, 1890.

DON'T MISS
THE
Grand Military Tournament
AT THE
Biggleswade Fête,
AUGUST BANK HOLIDAY.

WITH
MILITARY TRAINED HORSES
As used in the Tournament at the Agricultural Hall, Islington.

Band of Her Majesty's "SCOTS GUARDS,"
BICYCLE & FLAT RACES, &c.,
OBSTACLE RACE ON HORSEBACK, &c., &c.

THE WHOLE ENTAILING AN EXPENDITURE OF UPWARDS OF £350.

ADMISSION TO GROUNDS—1s. after 4 o'clock 6d.
CHEAP TICKETS UP TO WEDNESDAY, 30th JULY.

ENORMOUS GRAND STAND,
Tickets for which should be purchased of SPONG & SON, at once, in order to secure a seat
PRICES 2s. 6d. (Limited), 1s. 6d. and 1s.

While the Victorian army policed the British Empire the public were kept entertained at home, as this programme for a military fête at Biggleswade on 4 August 1890 shows. According to the *Bedfordshire Times* men from several cavalry regiments, watched by a crowd of between 10,000 and 12,000 people, carried out a fencing display that included 'cutting a whole sheep in two by one clean stroke'.

Pioneers of the 1st Battalion, the Bedfordshire Regiment, in India at the time of the Relief of Chitral Expedition. In 1895 the Pathan tribesmen on the North West Frontier revolted and barred the way to the British outpost at Chitral. The 1st Bedfords formed part of the force that successfully relieved the garrison.

Lance-corporal of the 3rd Volunteer Battalion, the Bedfordshire Regiment, *c.* 1900. The Battalion was formed locally in 1887 as a successor to the Bedfordshire Rifle Volunteer Corps established in 1859–60, and was in turn superseded by the 5th Battalion, the Bedfordshire Regiment (Territorials) in 1908. Some men from the 3rd Volunteer Battalion served in the South African War of 1899–1902. Several died of disease.

War with South Africa was declared on 11 October 1899, the culmination of a long-running dispute over political representation and the mineral wealth of the Republic. This photograph was taken outside Luton Town Hall, probably at the end of 1899, but the precise occasion is unknown. It could show a recruiting drive, given the posters calling up Luton reservists and the veteran with his campaign medal in the centre of the picture.

Major John Stanley Lightfoot at camp at Bloemfontein, South Africa, in May 1900. Thanks to faulty staff work the 2nd Battalion Bedfordshire Regiment were bivouacked on ground infected by enteric fever. Half the officers, including John Lightfoot, and one third of the other ranks went down with the disease. Lightfoot himself was invalided home and put on retired pay in 1903. His military career was not quite over as he was recruiting officer for Bedfordshire during the First World War. He died at Bedford in 1939.

The relief of Mafeking on 18 May 1900 was one of the turning points of the Boer War. The force commanded by Major-General Baden-Powell had been under siege since 13 October 1899 and when the garrison was relieved there was an outbreak of national rejoicing. At the village of Harrold the school children put the flags out (above) while the bellringers (below) rang a peal. First row, left to right: George Thew, F. Skevington. Second row: Charles Orpin, William Manton, C.F. Dinsley, Joseph McGrath. Back row: H. Munday, Frederick J. Bird, J.F. Lefevre, Frederick G. Crouch.

Biggleswade celebrated the Relief of Mafeking in style with a large procession which marched through the Market Square. Two companies of the British Boys' Brigade with a stretcher are in the centre of the photograph. All local children were given a packet of sweets, and houses, horses, vehicles and dogs were decorated with flags. When night fell there was a torchlight procession followed by fireworks. At Woburn the regulars assembled outside the Magpie Hotel (below). The placard on the soldier's decorated cycle refers to two other towns relieved in 1900: Kimberley (15 February) and Ladysmith (28 February). Several other parishes actually celebrated the end of the war, but there were still two years of fighting ahead.

Major Lord Alwyne Compton, DSO, commanded the 28th (Bedfordshire) Company, Imperial Yeomanry in South Africa. The regiment, popularly known as Compton's Horse, was raised in December 1899 when Lord Compton, MP for North Bedfordshire and son of the Marquess of Northampton, advertised for volunteer cavalry to serve abroad. About 120 men were recruited but of these only thirteen came from Bedfordshire. Lord Compton returned home in October 1900, relinquishing command of his depleted force to the Hon. F.C. Stanley. He died in 1912.

Bedford men pose with their Queen's South Africa Medals, 1901. Front row, left to right: John Roberts, 63rd Company, Imperial Yeomanry; Walter Peacock (1877–1957), Compton's Horse; Charles Stewart, 2nd Battalion, the Gordon Highlanders. Back row: Charles Peacock (1880–1976), Compton's Horse; Ted Foster, Compton's Horse; Albert Harrison, 56th Company, Imperial Yeomanry. Walter Peacock was the first volunteer to join Compton's Horse while his brother Charles was the county's last surviving veteran of the Boer War. In civilian life Walter formed the local firm of estate agents and auctioneers that still continues to this day. Charles was a dentist, remembered by many Bedfordians for his habit of asking patients to join him in prayer before treatment.

When peace was signed in South Africa on
31 May 1902 it was time for people to celebrate
and soldiers like John Sinfield of Aspley Guise
(right) to return home. There was another
opportunity for rejoicing when General Sir John
French visited Bedford on 24 July 1902. The
Bedfordshire Imperial Yeomanry (above)
provided part of the escort as the procession
passed along the High Street.

EDWARDIAN SUNSET,
1901–1914

The South African war memorial at Bedford was unveiled by Lady Cowper on 2 June 1904. The 230 names included soldiers who had served in Bedfordshire regiments and local men in other branches of the forces.

The 1st Battalion Bedfordshire Regiment on manoeuvres in the West Country in 1910, idyllic scenes
compared to the slaughter and hardship of the First World War. Troops halt for tea by a village post office
(above) while at camp, men waiting for the barber pose for the camera (below).

SOLDIERS' PAY.

INFANTRY.

After all stoppages for Messing and Washing have been deducted there remains, on an average, for the Soldier to spend as he chooses:—

	WEEKLY.	s.	d.
On joining		6	8½
After two years' service (if proficient and serving on an approved term of more than three years) 2nd Class ...		8	5½
1st Class		10	2½

In addition to above, Lodging, Food, Fuel, and Lighting are provided.

A Soldier in Hospital for wounds or illness contracted on Field Service, or injuries on Military Duty receives free Medical Treatment. In other circumstances a stoppage of 7d. for each day in Hospital is made, but in cases of sickness caused by Military Service one half of the stoppage is remitted.

The Messing Allowance, 3d a day, is also stopped when a Soldier is in Hospital except from injuries or sickness resulting from Active Service.

On Enlistment, a complete new Uniform and other Kit is issued free, and after 9 to 12 months' service quarterly allowance is given for the up-keep of Uniform and Kit. A careful Soldier benefits by any of the allowance he saves.

Men of good character are granted Furlough annually. While on furlough no stoppage is made for messing or washing, and the man receives 6d. a day in lieu of rations, the additional cash issue during furlough thus amounting to 5/6 a week.

A leaflet shewing terms of service, standards of height, age, &c., can be obtained at any Post Office or Barracks in the United Kingdom, or from any Recruiter.

God Save the King.

THE BEDFORDSHIRE REGIMENT.

Gone for a soldier. A recruiting postcard for the Bedfordshire Regiment (above) and a poster outside Langford post office (below), *c.* 1910. Advertisements like these encouraged men to enlist in the regular forces, while the creation of the Territorial Army in 1908 meant increased opportunities for part-time soldiering.

The Aldershot Oven

The Aldershot oven is very easily erected, it takes four men about forty five minutes to erect one, when once everything is ready, It consists of 2 half circles 1 bottom, 2 ends, 4 Bars, 9 tins, 1 peel

Weight about 3½ cwts

See Page 20

The oven will bake 108 1¼ loaves in one batch, It requires from 150 to 200 lbs of wood to heat it when once it has been dried

A page from the cookery book compiled by Corporal W. Davis of the Bedfordshire Militia who attended the School of Cookery at Aldershot in 1909. The army diet still lacked fresh produce and consisted largely of bread, potatoes, meat and tea.

The annual camp is a feature of life in the Territorial Army. Here soldiers of the 5th Battalion, Bedfordshire Regiment, are assembled for church parade at Felixstowe, 1907 (above) and for their morning ablutions at Ipswich in 1910 (below).

General Sir Henry Redvers Buller VC (1839–1908), Commander-In-Chief in South Africa in 1899–1900, opened Toddington Rifle Range on 25 October 1907. Buller fired the first shot and got a bull's eye, but most of the villagers thought the result had been fixed. The range was built to provide shooting practice for local men, but soon fell into disuse. In the lower picture Buller is the man standing left of the centre, his face obscuring that of the lady behind him.

Troopers checking and cleaning their saddles and equipment at the Bedfordshire Imperial Yeomanry camp, Wrest Park, Silsoe, 1905. The camp lasted a fortnight (31 May–15 June) while the men were put through their paces, with reveille at 5.30 a.m and coffee at 6 a.m. followed by at least an hour grooming the horses before breakfast at 7.30 a.m. After morning parade the troopers took part in mounted and foot drills and in war-games with the militia encamped at Ampthill.

The veteran. Charles William Emery (c. 1879–1958) poses with his horse Panther at Bedford cattle market, c. 1912. He is wearing his medals for the South African War.

In the period before the First World War conditions for soldiers in the ranks gradually improved. Sergeants of the 1st Bedfords relax in their mess at Aden (above) while the battalion was on garrison duty there, *c*. 1907. The lower picture shows the refreshment room of the 2nd Battalion, *c*. 1910, with tinned food stored behind the bar at the far end.

FIRST WORLD WAR,
1914–1919

A call to arms. By 1916, Britain's regular and territorial armies had been largely destroyed and Lord Kitchener appealed for recruits. At Sandy local veterans publicised the campaign by posing on the steps of the Victory Cinema in Bedford Road. They were (left to right): Sidney Stacey (unit unknown); Frederick James Braybrooks (7th Bedfords, killed 1917); Frederick Charles Spring (2nd Bedfords, won the Military Medal in 1917); Herbert John Gammons (7th Bedfords, killed 1917, won the Military Medal); Herbert George Addison (6th Bedfords, killed 1917); Sidney Braybrooks (lieutenant, Royal Sussex Regt, later in the Labour Corps, died of pneumonia 1919); Albert William Finding (Royal Garrison Artillery); Clifford Finding (7th Bedfords, wounded 1917); Victor Wagstaff (7th Bedfords, wounded 1916); Frederick John Page (Bedfords); Charles Payne (Bedfords); Frederick Huckle (unit unknown).

The chance meeting of the 1st and 2nd Battalions of the Bedfordshire Regiment at Locre on 6 November 1914 is commemorated in this oil painting by Joseph Gray. The headquarters and two companies of the 1st Battalion, which were travelling in London buses on their way to Ypres, encountered the remnants of the 2nd Battalion resting by the roadside. The 2nd Battalion had helped stem the German rush for the Channel ports, but at a terrible cost, losing three-quarters of its strength.

The billeting of thousands of Highland territorials in Bedford between August 1914 and Spring 1915 was one of the most memorable events in the county town during the First World War. In the upper picture troops march down De Parys Avenue past John Bunyan's statue, August 1914. Soldiers practise sword-dancing outside their billet (below). The Highlanders were very popular in the town, but memories were clouded by a measles epidemic which struck many of them down.

A soldier's life was not all drudgery and hardship, with the risk of death, wounds or disease in the field. There were organised sports such as the Highland dancing competition in Bedford Park in 1915 (above) as well as other amusements (below).

In August 1914 the local territorial battalion, the 1st/5th Battalion, Bedfordshire Regiment was mobilised, while in September the 2nd/5th Battalion was raised as a draft-finding unit. Both battalions spent long periods in training and on the march. Exhaustion is etched on the faces of the men of the 2nd/5th Bedfords fallen out by the roadside (above). The field kitchen belongs to the A or Bedford Company of the 1st/5th Bedfords (below).

On 5 June 1915 the 1st/5th Battalion, Bedfordshire Regiment, was given a mayoral reception at Luton, prior to embarkation for Gallipoli on 26 July. The mayor welcomed the men from a platform outside the town hall (above). After the reception they marched down George Street (below) watched by a large crowd.

An army marches on its stomach. Feeding the mass armies of the First World War required catering on a huge

scale. This field bakery was in Ampthill Road, Bedford, on a site popularly known as the ballast hole, *c.* 1916.

Soldiers could rely on their often monotonous army rations, but had to carry out most other chores themselves. Here, men are washing their clothes outside Waller Street Wesleyan Methodist Chapel in Luton town centre, *c.* 1916.

In March 1916 severe gales brought down trees all over Bedfordshire. These soldiers are picking their way through the fallen trees near Luton Hoo Park.

Firms of publishers and stationers were quick to
see the opportunities presented by a war which
kept soldiers and their womenfolk apart for long
periods (right). At Potton a motor bus was hired
to convey volunteers for Lord Kitchener's army
to Bedford in 1916 (below).

Recruits of the 5th Battalion Bedfordshire Regiment in training at Landguard Camp, Felixstowe, in 1915. The emphasis was often on hand-to-hand combat using the bayonet or (as here) the rifle butt, but in reality most soldiers were killed by shells or bullets fired by a distant enemy.

During the First World War the towns and villages of Bedfordshire became busy with troops on the march. The photograph shows a horse-drawn team in Shefford High Street, *c.* 1916. They may be carrying cable-laying equipment for the Royal Engineers.

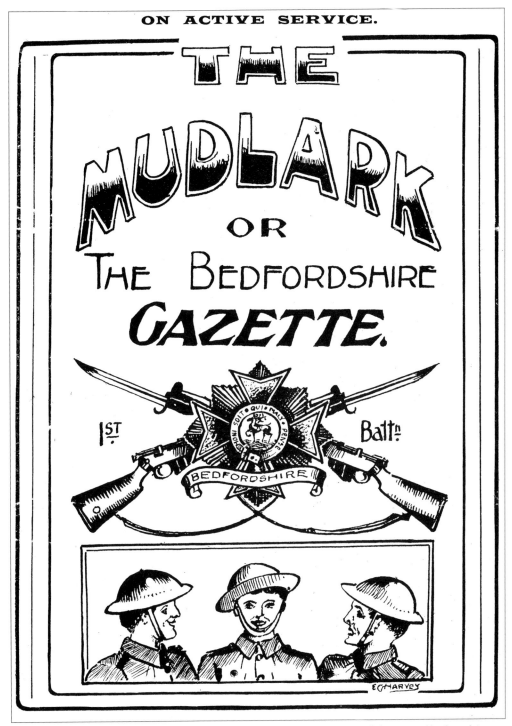

The Mudlark magazine was first produced in April 1916 to entertain men of the 1st Bedfords and 'annoy the Hun to distraction should it be unfortunate enough to fall into his hands'. The magazine did not last long and probably ceased publication when censorship was tightened up following the terrible losses during the Battle of the Somme.

Unofficial photography was forbidden at the
Front and surviving examples are rare. Captain
Geoffrey Anstee of the 1st Bedfords took this
photograph of his runner, Private Palmer, in the
Polderhoek Sector of the Western Front in
December 1917.

Most so-called 'action' photographs were
carefully posed with the enemy nowhere in sight.
Here soldiers of the 5th Bedfords pose with a
machine-gun used for anti-aircraft work when the
battalion was fighting the Turks at Mejdal Yaba,
Palestine, in 1918.

An embroidered and beaded heart sent by a soldier at the Front to his family at home. The design often included a regimental badge (as here) or a portrait photograph. Its actual size is about seven inches across by six inches at its widest points.

Second Air Mechanic Victor Harding of Stevington (1894–1955) served as a sheet metal worker with the 12th Squadron Royal Flying Corps (RAF from April 1918) on the Western Front from 1915 to 1918. The flying kit and helmet are perhaps photographer's props borrowed for the occasion.

Laura Millard of Meppershall served in the Women's Royal Air Force during the war, probably at nearby RAF Henlow. She married Ernest Bland, an ironmonger from Shefford, on 3 August 1914, the day before war was declared.

Fund raising at Stotfold, 1915. Hospital Day at Stotfold (above) was first held in 1914 to raise extra funds for the hospital and in the following year the National Deposit Friendly Society float was part of the parade. At the same time a collection of fruit and vegetables was made for the Navy (below).

POTTON

PUBLIC WARNING.

When Zeppelins are reported to be in this district, all House=holders are requested to assist the Police by **at once Extinguishing any Light that is visible from the outside of any House or Shop,** and all persons are asked to remain indoors.

Messrs F. W. Braybrooks have arranged for the Hooter at their Works to give Five Blasts in quick succession as a warning to the public.

F. W. BRAYBROOKS,

Chairman Potton Parish Council.

R. ELPHICK, PRINTER, POTTON.

During the First World War civilians suffered from air raids for the first time. Unlike London and parts of the east coast, Bedfordshire was not badly hit, but in March 1916 Potton Parish Council were sufficiently concerned to issue this notice. Frederick Braybrooks, Chairman of the Council, arranged for the hooter at his leather and parchment works to sound zeppelin warnings.

Forty-two Vickers Vimy bombers were built by
Morgans Works at Linslade (above) during the
war. The bodies of the aeroplanes, minus their
wings, were taken through the nearby town of
Leighton Buzzard, reassembled at Scott's Field
and flown off to various aerodromes. Local girls
(left to right) Doris Troughton, May Dimmock
and Nell Underwood were employed at the
Works. The site of the factory is now occupied
by a Tesco supermarket.

Workers at James Robinson's Leighton Buzzard factory making basketwork shell casings, *c.* 1916.

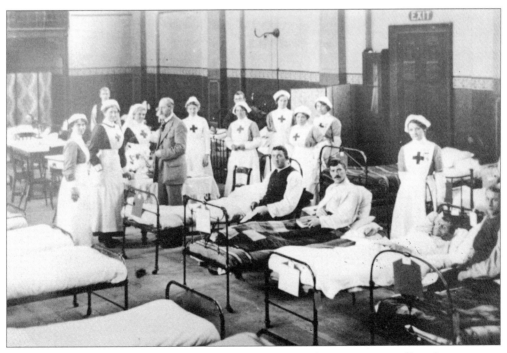

Leighton Buzzard Corn Exchange was used as a hospital during the war. Doctor William Square (centre left, standing) poses with staff and patients, *c.* 1916.

Wartime visitors. The Doms family (right), refugees from the German invasion of Belgium in 1914, found shelter with Mrs Bradstow of Odell. In happier circumstances, King George V and Queen Mary visited Bedford on 27 June 1918, where they toured the Queen's Engineering Works, the High School for Girls and Bedford School. The civic reception (below) was held at the Town Hall where the members of the waiting committee were so keyed-up that the sound of a Corporation dustcart was initially taken for the approach of the royal party.

On 6 January 1919 a banquet was held at Bedford Corn Exchange for 184 repatriated prisoners of war. Each man received a pocket knife and case inscribed with the date of the Armistice, 11 November 1918, as a souvenir.

The demobilisation of the troops meant the end of the work of the Bedford War Hospital Supply Depot which met for the last time on 31 January 1919. Since January 1916 these redoubtable Bedford ladies had made 18,692 garments for Serbian refugees, various battalions of the Bedfordshire Regiment, and the British and French branches of the Red Cross.

BETWEEN THE WARS, 1919–1939

Peace Souvenirs, 1919. The carrier bag, which once held a bun and an orange, was given to Bedford schoolchildren on 3 July 1919. Luton children were to be presented with a medal, a gift from the mayor Henry Impey, but they were not ready for distribution until mid-August, when the youngsters were on their summer holidays. (The medal shown lacks a ribbon and suspension bar.)

The return of the 1st Bedfords. On 28 April 1919 Bedford welcomed a contingent of about fifty men of the battalion, all that remained of the original unit mobilised in 1914. The troops are marching along Midland Road prior to a service at St Paul's Church, a civic reception, and lunch at the Corn Exchange.

The signing of the Armistice did not mean rapid demobilisation for many troops. On 4 December 1918 the 5th Bedfords left Beirut for Egypt as part of the Egyptian Expeditionary Force and by April 1919 they were on lorry patrol during the rebellion in Cairo. The battalion had to wait until 4 August 1919 for their 'welcome home' reception at Bedford.

Peace celebrations, 19 July 1919. Most towns and villages celebrated Peace Day with a procession of floats, as at Dunstable (above). At Toddington (below) the firemen decorated their 1832 pattern engine. Fred Taylor, the local coalman, is holding the horse's head.

PEACE DAY TODDINGTON. JULY 19. 1919   27.   KAY PHOTO

The Luton Peace Day procession (above) was the prelude to a riot that left the town hall a burnt-out ruin (below). The Borough Council was already unpopular, but their refusal to allow demobilised ex-servicemen to hold a drumhead memorial service in Wardown Park was the final straw. When the procession halted at the town hall the Councillors were showered with missiles and nearby shops looted. That evening the town hall was set on fire. The mayor Henry Impey escaped through a back entrance disguised as a special constable.

After the First World War memorials were erected in towns and villages all over Bedfordshire. Bletsoe war memorial, a Celtic Cross in grey granite bearing the names of eleven men who fell in action, was unveiled on 13 June 1920. The Hon. Moubray St John unveiled the memorial while the Rev. Percy Underhill conducted the service. Corporal Noble sounded the Last Post and Reveille.

Eaton Bray war memorial was unveiled by the Lord Lieutenant, Mr S. Howard Whitbread, on 31 July 1921. The cross is built mainly of red and grey Scottish granite and commemorates thirty-three men who died during the conflict.

Armistice Day at Leighton Buzzard, 1919. Boy Scouts mount guard on the temporary war memorial put up in front of the Market Cross.

The permanent war memorial at Leighton Buzzard is reputed to be the largest block of granite ever mined in the British Isles. The monolith, 25 feet 3 inches high and weighing 22 tons, took three days to erect on the site in Church Square. It was unveiled by Lord Ampthill on 11 November 1920.

Leighton Buzzard war memorial in the 1920s. The names of the 171 local men killed in the First World War are inscribed around the sides. After the Second World War a further 51 names were added to the block above the base stone.

The band of the 2nd Battalion Bedfordshire and Hertfordshire Regiment strikes up as the Governor arrives at Poona Races in the autumn of 1923. After the First World War the Regiment (created in July 1919 from the amalgamation of the Bedfordshire and Hertfordshire Regiments) resumed its role of policing the Empire. The 2nd Battalion served in India between 1919 and 1925, and then in Iraq in 1925–6 before returning home after nineteen years of nearly continuous foreign service.

The Prince of Wales, the future Edward VIII, presented new Colours and a set of eleven silver drums to the 2nd Battalion Bedfordshire and Hertfordshire Regiment at Luton football ground on 17 November 1926. On the following afternoon the old Colours were laid up in St Paul's Church, Bedford.

In 1927–28 the 1st Battalion Bedfordshire and Hertfordshire Regiment formed part of the Shanghai Defence Force, an international force – although mostly British – sent to protect the trade of the port from the Chinese Nationalists. In May 1928 the battalion moved by rail to Kuyeh where its armoured train was used to protect the mines of the Kilan Mining Association. The Association later presented the battalion with a silver model of the wagon shown in the photograph.

Those magnificent men in their flying machines. . . . Two views of RAF Henlow in the 1920s. Six parachutists drop from the wing tips of Vickers Vimy bombers during a rehearsal for a display on 1 June 1929 (above). The interior of the hangar (below) shows a selection of mostly Avro fighters built in 1918–19.

Between the wars the various local units of the Territorial Army went on their annual training as usual. The photograph shows the pay parade of the 105th (Bedfs. Yeomanry) Field Brigade, Royal Artillery, at Roedean Forest, Sussex, in the 1930s.

Both battalions of the Bedfordshire and Hertfordshire Regiment served during the Arab revolts in Palestine, the 2nd Battalion in 1936 and the 1st Battalion in 1938–9. An unusual innovation was the Ford V8 pick-up, adapted for travel on the railway as a patrol car, and shown here being inspected by men of C Company, 2nd Battalion, at Tulkarm, in 1936.

Aerial view of the Regimental Depot, Bedfordshire and Hertfordshire Regiment, 1936. This view of Kempston Barracks from the south-west shows Spring Road on the left and Bedford Road beyond the main building in the distance. The amalgamation of the Regiment with the 1st Battalion Essex Regiment in 1958 made the Depot virtually redundant and it finally closed in September 1977. Much of the site has been redeveloped for housing, but the left hand portion of the keep, including the main tower, still survives.

SECTION SIX

SECOND WORLD WAR, 1939–1945

IMPORTANT NOTICE

BOROUGH OF LUTON

AIR RAID PRECAUTIONS
Night of 8-9th July, 1939

Your Council have agreed to hold a "Black-out" on the night of 8/9th July, 1939, and it is desired to secure that no lights are visible from the air between midnight and four o'clock in the morning of 9th July, 1939.

The darkening of areas exposed to air attack may be expected to be an essential feature of the defence of this country in time of war, and useful information on the best means of effecting this may be derived from the present Exercise.

HOUSEHOLDERS AND ALL OTHER OCCUPIERS OF PREMISES ARE ACCORDINGLY ASKED TO ASSIST BY ENSURING THAT LIGHTS IN THEIR PREMISES ARE EXTINGUISHED OR SCREENED BY DARK CURTAINS OR BLINDS, BETWEEN MIDNIGHT AND FOUR O'CLOCK IN THE EARLY MORNING OF 9th JULY, 1939. IT IS PARTICULARLY DESIRABLE THAT EXTERNAL LIGHTS AND OTHER LIGHTS DIRECTLY VISIBLE FROM THE SKY SHOULD BE EXTINGUISHED OR SCREENED.

As lighting in streets will be restricted, vehicles should, so far as possible, keep off the roads during the darkened period.

It is emphasised that there is no intention, in connection with the "Black-out," of cutting off lighting or power supplies at the mains.

W. H. ROBINSON, Town Clerk.

As the war clouds gathered Luton practised the blackout, soon to become a reality when war was declared on 3 September 1939.

In 1939 36,000 evacuees, mostly from London
and its suburbs, were billeted in Bedfordshire.
During 1–3 September 7,000 mothers and
children arrived at Leighton Buzzard station
(left). Billeting went smoothly, but extra
bedding and blankets had to be commandeered
from local shops as Government supplies failed
to arrive. At Bedford (below) some of the
17,000 evacuees allotted to the Borough pass
the Royal County Theatre in Midland Road.

Children queue outside the Regal cinema, Biggleswade, for a showing of the film *Suez* starring Tyrone Power and Loretta Young, September 1939. On the outbreak of war cinemas were closed, but quickly reopened partly to cater for the evacuees. Air raid precautions were strict and performances had to finish by 10 p.m.

Bedford men registering for war service under the Conscription Act, 12 December 1939.

When the petrol shortage started to bite, ingenious contraptions were devised to convert vehicles to gas. Predictably, Bedford District Gas Company were among the first to convert their vans in April 1940 (above). By 1942 some Luton buses (below) towed burners for producing gas, but the vehicles needed continual maintenance and often got stuck on steep gradients. By 1943 many companies were converting buses back to petrol.

Scrap metal salvage. Aluminium utensils were collected to make into aeroplanes: this street collection is pictured at the junction of The Bank and London Road, Biggleswade in July 1940 (above). The Mayor of Bedford, at the request of the Ministry of Supply, appealed to local residents to give up their iron railings and gates for munitions. These railings are being removed from Bushmead Avenue in July 1941(below).

Make Do and Mend. This advertisement for the Invisible Mending and Hosiery Repair Company, run by Czech Mr J. Finger of Bedford, appeared in 1941.

Paper salvage at Bedford. Paper recycling was encouraged during the war. Miss Audrey Howard of Clapham Park and her party are shown packing waste paper in April 1941 (above). In July 1942 there was a propaganda drive for a Mile of Books. The collectors are shown in De Parys Avenue.

The differences of scale in collecting scrap metal for salvage in town and country are apparent in these two photographs. The upper picture shows collecting in progress at the village of Maulden in July 1940 while at Luton (below) the Corporation dustcart turned out to help, *c*. 1942.

Women at War. When war broke out women were mobilised as never before to serve on the home front. On 1 June 1940 the Bedfordshire Women's Land Army paraded in Bedford (above) hoping to attract volunteers. The organisation swelled from 85 volunteers in 1939 to well over 1,000 by 1944.

In the summer of 1942 there was a big recruitment drive for women. This switchboard operator was on the staff of the Women's Auxiliary Police at Bedford.

Bedfordshire prepares for air attack. This
snapshot view (left) shows shelters under
construction at Luton probably for Skefko Ball
Bearing Co. Ltd of Leagrove Road, *c.* 1941. At
Bedford the bells of St Paul's Church (below)
were removed for safe-keeping in September
1941 and stored in a corner of the churchyard.

Air raid precautions and the work of local fire brigades were vital in reducing the damage caused by enemy bombs. A firewatcher spots for fire bombs or flares at Luton in September 1940 (right) while Ampthill Fire Brigade pose by their engine in May 1941 (below). In 1941 the National Fire Service was formed, enabling brigades to be transferred to London, county and other blitzed areas to assist firefighters there.

Luton, with its Vauxhall car plant and other major industries, suffered more from bombing than any other place in Bedfordshire: 107 people were killed and nearly 500 injured. The first raid occurred without warning and in daylight on 30 August 1940 when Vauxhall Motors was hit. Many houses like those at Russell Rise (above) were destroyed. On 22 September a parachute mine fell in front of the Park Street bus depot (below) injuring six employees and destroying forty-six buses and half a million tickets.

Once the 'all-clear' sounded wardens and householders saved what they could from ruined buildings. These photographs show the aftermath of a raid on the Park Street area of Luton in September 1940. Approximately 7,000 buildings were destroyed or damaged in Luton during the war and many people were made homeless.

Bedfordshire lacked heavy anti-aircraft defences but occasionally enemy aircraft were brought down and displayed as war trophies. A policeman and a Home Guard officer, watched by a crowd of boys, inspect a German fighter at Luton, 7 December 1940.

Bedford's worst raid occurred on 23 July 1942 when ten people were killed. Civil Defence personnel sift through the rubble of the Grosvenor Hotel at 5–7 Ashburnham Road, half of which has collapsed like a pack of cards.

ACHTUNG!
ACHTUNG!
ACHTUNG!

Mine goot freund Herr Gobbles, has this morning to me told that Luton are a War Weapons Week having. My patients is exhausted.

I demand you not to save your money. If you two more destroyers buy, they will sink my U Boats which are guarding the seas, and challenge my new orders for everybody, everywhere. And you know how I have been "protecting" the Danes, the Norwegians, the Dutch and the Belgians as well as the Czechs and the Poles. I want to "protect" you and the Americans and everybody else on earth,

It will to me be a great blow if you your million pounds get.

ADOLF

Issued in spite of Hitler, by the Publicity Sub-Committee Luton War Weapons Week.
Keep this, it may be valuable.
Printed at the Leagrave Press by Gibbs, Bamforth & Co. (Luton) Ltd., Luton

One of the 20,000 satirical leaflets dropped from the air on the Luton and Dunstable area during War Weapons Week, 1941. The two towns, together with the villages in the Luton Rural District, combined to raise one million pounds in a week for the war effort. In the event over £1,400,000 was raised, enough for three destroyers, but people were disappointed that none of the vessels was named after local towns.

War Weapons Week. The mayor and a large crowd watch as a tank passes Dunstable town hall during a procession held in March 1941 (above). The Chief Constable of Bedfordshire, Commander William Willis, is taking the salute. At Leighton Buzzard a large target indicator was put up in Church Square (left).

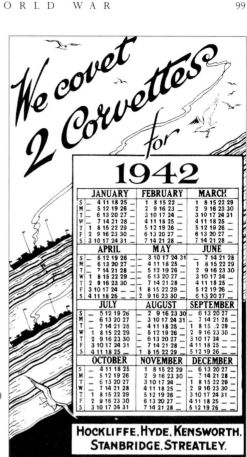

We covet 2 Corvettes for

1942

	JANUARY	FEBRUARY	MARCH
S	— 4 11 18 25 —	1 8 15 22 —	1 8 15 22 29
M	— 5 12 19 26 —	2 9 16 23 —	2 9 16 23 30
T	— 6 13 20 27 —	3 10 17 24 —	3 10 17 24 31
W	— 7 14 21 28 —	4 11 18 25 —	4 11 18 25 —
T	1 8 15 22 29 —	5 12 19 26 —	5 12 19 26 —
F	2 9 16 23 30 —	6 13 20 27 —	6 13 20 27 —
S	3 10 17 24 31	7 14 21 28 —	7 14 21 28 —

	APRIL	MAY	JUNE
S	— 5 12 19 26 —	3 10 17 24 31	— 7 14 21 28
M	— 6 13 20 27 —	4 11 18 25 —	1 8 15 22 29
T	— 7 14 21 28 —	5 12 19 26 —	2 9 16 23 30
W	1 8 15 22 29 —	6 13 20 27 —	3 10 17 24 —
T	2 9 16 23 30 —	7 14 21 28 —	4 11 18 25 —
F	3 10 17 24 —	1 8 15 22 29 —	5 12 19 26 —
S	4 11 18 25 —	2 9 16 23 30	6 13 20 27 —

	JULY	AUGUST	SEPTEMBER
S	— 5 12 19 26	2 9 16 23 30	— 6 13 20 27
M	— 6 13 20 27	3 10 17 24 31	— 7 14 21 28
T	— 7 14 21 28	4 11 18 25 —	1 8 15 22 29
W	1 8 15 22 29	5 12 19 26 —	2 9 16 23 30
T	2 9 16 23 30	6 13 20 27 —	3 10 17 24 —
F	3 10 17 24 31	7 14 21 28 —	4 11 18 25 —
S	4 11 18 25 —	1 8 15 22 29	5 12 19 26 —

	OCTOBER	NOVEMBER	DECEMBER
S	— 4 11 18 25	1 8 15 22 29	— 6 13 20 27
M	— 5 12 19 26	2 9 16 23 30	— 7 14 21 28
T	— 6 13 20 27	3 10 17 24 —	1 8 15 22 29
W	— 7 14 21 28	4 11 18 25 —	2 9 16 23 30
T	1 8 15 22 29	5 12 19 26 —	3 10 17 24 31
F	2 9 16 23 30	6 13 20 27 —	4 11 18 25 —
S	3 10 17 24 31	7 14 21 28 —	5 12 19 26 —

HOCKLIFFE, HYDE, KENSWORTH, STANBRIDGE, STREATLEY.

As an inland county Bedfordshire lacks a strong naval tradition but the 1942 Warships Week campaign was still enthusiastically supported (right). A few ships were named after local towns and villages, including HMS *Oakley* (below), a Hunt Class destroyer of 1,050 tons launched in January 1942. During her wartime career she served on escort duty and anti-U-boat patrols and took part in the allied landing at Sicily on 10 July 1943.

American troops parade down the High Street at the start of Bedford's Salute the Soldier Week on 9 June 1944. During a week of festivities and fund-raising to celebrate D-Day people were encouraged to invest in Savings Certificates, Defence Bonds and National War Bonds.

Thurleigh was the home of the 306th Bombardment Group of the 8th American Air Force between September 1942 and December 1945. A Flying Fortress is loaded with incendiary bombs prior to a raid in 1943.

Thurleigh airfield, *c.* 1943. American airmen assemble on the control tower awaiting the return of bombers from a raid (above). After the raid, medics (below) would assist injured aircrew. Bill Houlihan (adjusting bandages on the casualty's head) was a medical assistant at the base from 1942 to 1945.

Glenn Miller (above, second from right, at the Granada Theatre, November 1944) and David Niven
(below, at the Corn Exchange, July 1944) were two stars who visited Bedford during the war. Glenn
Miller's name in particular is indelibly associated with Bedfordshire. His band was evacuated to Bedford
from London soon after D-Day and shared facilities at the Corn Exchange with the BBC Symphony
Orchestra under Sir Adrian Boult. Radio schedules and tours kept the band busy between July and
December, but Miller disappeared without trace on 15 December 1944 on a flight from Twinwoods,
Clapham, to Paris where he had planned to make a Christmas broadcast.

Soldiers of the 2nd Battalion, Bedfordshire and Hertfordshire Regiment, advancing through a ruined village in Italy, 1944. The 2nd Battalion served in north-west Africa and Egypt between March 1943 and February 1944 before transferring to Italy where it took part in the successful attack on Cassino. In December the Battalion moved to Greece in order to support the Regent's government against the Communists, where it remained for the rest of the war.

Kenneth Wildman of Bedford (1914–1973) served with the Royal West Kent Regiment in Burma. This well-worn photograph shows Chindits outside the Shand Road Coffee Shop at Maubin, *c.* 1944. Private Wildman is second from right in the seated group, with a child on his knee.

The capture of thousands of British and Commonwealth troops by the Japanese at the fall of Singapore in February 1942 was one of the disasters of the Second World War. Regimental Sergeant-Major Laurence Dunham was taken prisoner with the 5th Battalion Bedfordshire and Hertfordshire Regiment and was a prisoner-of-war in Thailand when this portrait was painted in 1945. Over 200 men of the battalion died during their captivity.

Despite the privations of captivity under the Japanese some soldiers showed remarkable resilience and recorded their experiences. This water-colour shows Thai women pouring baskets of rice into a tub, c. 1944.

Demob. Flight-Sergeant Nevil J. Millard of Bedford, who was called up early in 1939, was the first man serving in the RAF to report at Cardington for demobilization in June 1945. Each serviceman was entitled to a suit, a tie, a shirt and two collars, a pair of socks and shoes, and a hat and a raincoat.

Two hours later Mr. Millard had been fitted out with civilian clothes and was taking a walk in Bedford High Street. He returned to his old job at the Igranic Electric Co. Ltd.

The Garden of Remembrance at Biggleswade market square, September 1945. The war memorial was subsequently moved from the Shortmead Street and High Street junction to this site.

PEACE CELEBRATIONS, 1945–1946

Victory in Europe Day, 8 May 1945. The residents of Kirkman Close, Bedford, celebrate in style. The people include David Morris (far left, in braces), Joe Tenby (fiddle player), Mrs Tenby (in centre, wearing rosette) and Frank Charteress (at the piano).

Balmoral Avenue VE Day celebrations. Cedric Collard, the Borough Treasurer, took a snapshot of the street party in this small Bedford cul-de-sac. The men (standing, left to right) are Richard Marks, Cecil Austin, Ernest Page, Fred Cockman, and Alfred Beard. The seated women are Mrs Thompson (at head of table) and far side (left to right) Mrs Beard, Ada Collard, Jean Butters, Mrs Ibbott (a visitor), Violet Page, Phyllis Marks, Doris Austin and Frances Cockman. Fred Cockman, then a 43-year-old manager of a small insurance office, remembers: 'We men set up the tables, putting them end to end along the road. The ladies brought out their table cloths and cakes. In my road people were never more than formally polite, but that day all reserve was broken down and there was an upsurge of warm friendship which was perfectly genuine.'

VE Day. Bedford Land Army girls celebrated in St Paul's Square (above), while at Biggleswade couples danced in Hitchin Street (below). The merrymaking continued into the early hours of the following morning.

At Luton a large crowd assembled at the war memorial on VE Day (left). Elsewhere in the town youngsters were happy to hang Hitler in effigy (below).

The VJ Day celebrations in August 1945 marked the end of all hostilities and were followed by another wave of rejoicing. At Lidlington there was a street party (above). Stewartby residents danced round an effigy of Hitler before setting light to the bonfire (below).

The childrens' fancy dress parade off Cardington Road, Bedford, on VJ Day. There are a number of

imaginative costumes including 'Hitler' holding a copy of *Mein Kampf*.

Another event of 1945 was the Red Cross victory parade at Biggleswade on 2 June. This decorated NAAFI mobile canteen took part in the procession through the centre of the town.

On 8 June 1946 Bedfordshire celebrated Victory Day in spite of bad weather. After the judging of the fancy dress parade at Ampthill the children marched through the streets to the park. The procession was headed by former members of the old Town Band.

On 14 February 1946 the nineteen-year-old Princess Elizabeth (right) visited Bedford to open an exhibition on agricultural work and handicrafts held by the Bedfordshire Women's Land Army. Six hundred members of the Land Army marched past the podium in St Paul's Square (below). The celebrations continued over the next two days with a BBC concert, conducted in part by Trevor Howard, a fun-fair and dancing at the Corn Exchange.

EATON BRAY VICTORY CELEBRATIONS

SATURDAY, JUNE 8th., 1946.

OPENING CEREMONY AT 2 P.M.

on the Recreation Ground by the Vicar, REV. D. J. LAWRENCE.

≡ ≡ ≡

CARNIVAL PROCESSION

Judging to commence at 2.15 p.m. on the Recreation Ground.

≡ ≡ ≡

TEA FOR CHILDREN

(age 3 to 14 years).

In the National School at 3.45 p.m. Please bring your own mug. Followed by Tea for OLD PEOPLE. Cups of Tea will be available for others present as far as rations will allow.

≡ ≡ ≡

EVENING SPORTS TO COMMENCE at 5.45.

≡ ≡ ≡

BONFIRE AT 9.30 p.m.

≡ ≡ ≡

DANCE IN THE NATIONAL SCHOOL

FROM 9 P.M. TO 11.45   ADMISSION 1s.

It is hoped to have sufficient funds in hand after these Celebrations to erect a new set of swings for the children on the Recreation Ground.

Programme of the Eaton Bray victory celebrations, 8 June 1946.

THE LEGACY, POST 1945

At the end of the war Bedfordshire could start dismantling its blockhouses and ARP shelters. Here men are demolishing a pill box at Biggleswade, September 1945.

Yes, we have some bananas. Children gather round as the first post-war delivery of bananas arrives in Bedford, March 1946. Later police had to be called to one local shop to disperse a crowd of youngsters, many of whom had never seen a banana before. The stock of bananas was fairly distributed throughout the county: everyone under the age of eighteen could obtain 1 lb.

The post-war years were bleak ones, with virtually everything from coals to accommodation in short supply. In Bedford there was an acute shortage of coal in March 1946, aggravated by a run on the yards during a cold spell. Mrs Shreeves is shown taking her allowance of 28 lb which would have lasted less than a day in the average household.

Prefabricated houses at Leagrave, c. 1946. After the war prefabricated houses were built in large numbers, particularly in the Luton area, to accommodate bombed-out families.

Field Marshal Montgomery was a guest at Bedford School Speech Day on 28 June 1946. He is accompanied by the Headmaster Mr H. Grose-Hodge, and Sir Richard Wells, Chairman of the Governors. Monty also visited Bedford High School and attended the Bedford School old boys' dinner.

Despite the end of hostilities Bedfordshire's airfields were still busy, and there were occasional mishaps during training flights. Many acres of wheat were under threat when a Havard two-seater trainer from the Empire Test Pilots' School at Cranfield came down with engine trouble near Millbrook signal box on 29 July 1946. The crew, Lieutenant Giblin of the US Navy and Flight-Lieutenant Wallers, escaped unhurt.

The German prisoner-of-war camp at Clapham photographed when the War Office permitted a Press visit in August 1946. The 1,500 prisoners worked in the brickfields and on the land. Rations were below the quantities allowed for British civilians: a typical evening meal was meat and potato stew followed by a coarse porridge flavoured with cocoa powder.

Post-war austerity. A combination of rationing, power cuts and floods made 1947 a difficult year for many. Bedfordians responded to the Government's switch-off appeal in February and shopped by candlelight (above). In March there was flooding and hurricane damage all along the Great Ouse valley. Some buildings, like St Mary's Abbey Hotel, Bedford, were completely cut off by the flood water. The WVS meals on wheels service delivered hot meals to over 1,000 people marooned in their homes.

The Second World War memorial of the Bedfordshire and Hertfordshire Regiment was unveiled by Queen Elizabeth at Kempston on 11 November 1950. In the centre of the picture is the shrine containing the Book of Remembrance for more than 1,000 men of the regiment killed in the war.

Today, regimental and military museums in Britain play their part in keeping alive memories of war. Men of the Bedfordshire and Hertfordshire Regiment started collecting museum items in the 1920s, but the Regimental Museum at Kempston Barracks, shown here with the curator Major Eric Fanning in 1951, was not started until later. The museum was neglected when operations at the barracks were scaled down after 1958, but fortunately the collection, including militaria, uniforms and medals was later transferred to Luton Museum, Wardown Park, where it is now on display. The regimental papers and photographs are held by the County Record Office at Bedford.

The end of a tradition. The Bedfordshire and Hertfordshire Regiment mount guard at the opening of the Assizes in Bedford for the last time on 6 May 1958. Soon afterwards the regiment amalgamated with the Essex Regiment to form the 3rd East Anglian Regiment – and so passed into history.

The last Regimental Weekend of the Bedfordshire and Hertfordshire Regiment was held at Kempston Barracks on 7–8 June 1958. The guard, led by Lieutenant R. Dinnin, are dressed in the uniforms of 1688, the year the regiment was raised.

The derelict wireless studios at Milton Bryan in 1981. The studios were built in about 1942 in connection with a huge medium wave transmitter built at Crowborough, Sussex, by Department SO1 (Special Operations One). The transmitters were powerful enough to override enemy frequencies and transmit propaganda to the Germans. The first broadcasts from Milton Bryan were made on 5 February 1943 and were so authentic that many people believed them to be made by a genuine German forces radio.

Wartime relics. Underground air raid shelters near Dallow Road Infant School, Luton, were exposed during work on the A505 relief road in October 1988 (above). This pill box (below) in a back garden at Everton Road, Potton, pictured in October 1994, originally guarded a railway bridge on Myers Road. It now serves as a garden shed.

We will remember them. The Remembrance Day ceremony at Bedford war memorial, November 1995.

ACKNOWLEDGEMENTS

I would like to thank, on behalf of Bedfordshire Record office, all the people and organisations listed below who have donated or loaned the pictures which have made the book possible. I am also grateful to my colleagues at the Record Office for their help, especially Ruth Gill for word processing the text and Sue Edwards for carrying out some of the picture research. Dave Stubbs and Julian Markham of Bedfordshire County Council Photographic Services (sadly now closed) copied many of the pictures for the book and did an excellent job.

Finally, my thanks go to Doctor Peter Boyden and the staff of the National Army Museum for their patience in answering my queries about a few of the early illustrations.

My thanks to: Mrs D.W.M. Allen; Mr D. Armstrong; *Bedfordshire Times* Collection (at C.R.O.); Mrs P. Bickerdike; Biggleswade History Society (Liz Munns Collection); Mr P. Bixley; Cecil Higgins Art Gallery and Museum; Andrew Clark(e); Fred Cockman; Mr L.S. Dunham; Lady Errol; Ralph Franklin; Mrs J. Harris; Mrs M. How; Bill Knight; Rex Lancefield; Tom Lawson; Luton Museum (19, 53a, 56, 74a, 97: *Luton News* Collection at: 86b, 90b, 93b, 94–96a, 110, 119b); Mrs Manton; Mrs Morgan; Miss Peacock; Francis Pym; Frank Richards; Royal Anglian Regiment Archives; Mr P. Rutland; Mr L.A. Shelford; Miss S.A. Sinfield; David Stonebridge; Mrs J. Street; John Wainwright; Viv Willis; Richard Wildman; Mrs P.R. Yates.